Watching Over One Another in Love

Watching Over One Another in Love

A Wesleyan Model for Ministry Assessment

GWENDOLYNN PURUSHOTHAM

Revised Edition

GENERAL BOARD OF HIGHER EDUCATION AND MINISTRY
THE UNITED METHODIST CHURCH
NASHVILLE, TENNESSEE

The General Board of Higher Education and Ministry leads and serves The United Methodist Church in the recruitment, preparation, nurture, education, and support of Christian leaders—lay and clergy—for the work of making disciples of Jesus Christ for the transformation of the world. Its vision is that a new generation of Christian leaders will commit boldly to Jesus Christ and be characterized by intellectual excellence, moral integrity, spiritual courage, and holiness of heart and life.

The General Board of Higher Education and Ministry of The United Methodist Church is the church's agency for educational, institutional, and ministerial leadership. It serves as an advocate for the intellectual life of the church. The Board's mission embodies the Wesleyan tradition of commitment to the education of laypersons and ordained persons by providing access to higher education for all persons.

Contents

Acknowledgments

I am grateful to The United Methodist Church for teaching me the faith and giving me the privilege of serving as a layperson, pastor, district superintendent, and member of the staff at the General Board of Higher Education and Ministry of The United Methodist Church. All of these opportunities have contributed to my growth and learning. In many respects, this book is an outgrowth of all of these experiences.

I am especially appreciative of my colleagues at the General Board of Higher Education and Ministry, who provided support in the form of time, feedback, and funding for this project. In particular, I thank the staff in the Office of Interpretation for their expertise and work in the publication of this book.

A diverse group of persons reviewed the original manuscript at various stages in its development. Among them were laity, elders, deacons, bishops, and seminary professors. Reviewers were also diverse in their ethnic and racial backgrounds. Their feedback was enormously helpful and is reflected in these pages. I am indebted to them for their time and their input.

Julieanne Hallman and George Sinclair, Jr., former directors of Supervision and Field Education at Andover Newton Theological School, deserve special mention for teaching me the art of supervision through their competent practice and for the time they gave to provide extensive written and verbal feedback in the earliest stages of this project.

Long before this book was conceived, Kenneth Pohly developed, wrote about, and taught the concepts inherent in this process. His publications on the ministry of supervision and evaluation are primary sources of wisdom and inspiration for the covenantal model of ministry assessment and evaluation presented in this book. I am deeply grateful not only for his work but also for his personal encouragement in this endeavor.

It is one thing to write a book about ministry assessment; it is yet another to implement the principles and practices. Since the publication of *Watching Over One Another in Love* in 2007, Marilyn and Roger Evans, co-directors of the Pohly Center for Supervision and Leadership Formation at United Theological Seminary, Dayton, Ohio, have given wings to *Watching Over One Another in Love*. They have conducted numerous workshops with staff-parish relations committees, pastors, and district superintendents and have created companion resources to use with the book. One of these resources is included in the appendix of this revised edition.

My profound gratitude goes to Hendrik Pieterse, at the time Director of Scholarly Research and Book Editor for the General Board of Higher Education and Ministry. Henk guided, tended, and assisted in the creation of this book. His affirmation and critique instilled confidence even as it helped me improve upon my work. Henk embodies the principles and practices that are at the core of this model.

Finally, I thank my family: my parents, who lived to see the first edition of this book and with great pride even shared it with their elderly neighbors (as recommended reading!); my three amazing children, whose creativity, playfulness, and insight are sources of inspiration, delight, and wisdom; and my beloved Sam, who watches over so many in love and who encourages and cares for me every day.

— *Gwen Purushotham*

Introduction

"Support without accountability promotes moral weakness; accountability without support is a form of cruelty."[1]

This book arises out of a *need* and a *conviction*. The need is for a meaningful way to promote and hold together support and accountability in the practice of ministry. The conviction is that the engagement of persons in a process of ministry assessment grounded in a theology of grace and responsibility is a way to meet this urgent need in the church.

The need and the desire for holding together support and accountability with theological and spiritual integrity are pervasive in our churches. Questions and concerns pertaining to issues of accountability and support in ministry practice surface regularly in conversations with bishops, district superintendents, clergy, laity, boards of ordained ministry, local pastors, and ministry candidates. Accountability and support are the subject of national surveys as well as the topic of table conversation.

The words *accountability* and *support* carry connotations that evoke mixed responses in the context of ministry assessment and evaluation. On one side, some argue that more support and less accountability is what is needed to address issues of effectiveness in ministry practice. The word *accountability* conjures up feelings of defensiveness and resistance. It carries a connotation of being coerced by an outside authority to do something one would not do of one's own accord. It is associated with judgments and directives by observers or onlookers and with relationships that are more adversarial than supportive in nature.[2] Persons holding this view sometimes point to evaluative practices that have been disrespectful or harmful to pastors and staff. They point out that laypersons are often given responsibilities for ministries of support and accountability, without proper training. Thus, feelings of mistrust surround ministry assessment for both those who are evaluators and those whose ministry is evaluated. Rather than being viewed or experienced as a means of grace in which persons and congregations are formed for effective ministry, accountability measures are seen as a way to either satisfy an external requirement or manage ministers and ministry.

One the other side, for others *accountability* carries a more desirable connotation. Many laity and clergy perceive a lack of accountability, rather than too much, as the problem confronting the church. For them, too many persons serving in positions of leadership in the church are well supported but not held accountable for their effectiveness in ministry. Some complain about pastors who will not engage in reflection on their practice of ministry with laity (or peers) and who apparently are not required to do so by their district superintendents. Others point out that staff-parish relations committees are not clear about their role and do not take the initiative in providing a ministry of support and accountability.

Regardless of where persons find themselves in this debate, their responses reflect a common perception that support and accountability are at opposite ends of a pole, rather than two sides of a coin. This assumption (not always explicit but operative nonetheless) has led to attempts in the church to increase ministry effectiveness through placing a greater emphasis on *either* support *or* accountability rather than creating practices and fostering relationships that hold these two facets together.

Accountability and support issues tend to be focused around some common concerns and are expressed in questions such as the following:

- Where is the accountability?
- What is fair to expect of the pastor?
- Who are we to evaluate the pastor?
- Who are they to evaluate my ministry?
- What do they expect of me?
- What kind of support can I expect from them?
- How many chances are we going to give this pastor?
- How can we help ineffective pastors exit from ministry?
- What is the district superintendent going to do?
- Everyone agrees our pastor is doing a fine job. What is the point of doing a ministry assessment?
- Why should we meet if there is no problem?
- How can we tell our pastor that he (she) is not effective? It would hurt his (her) feelings.

Too often, confusion about the issues inherent in these questions, coupled with a lack of training, has resulted in a situation in which ministry assessment is done poorly, causing more harm than good, or is not done at all. The unfortunate outcome is that pastors and congregations do not assist one another in growing to the full stature of Christ, as God wills for us.

The following scenarios are not uncommon occurrences in the church:

Scenario 1

The district superintendent meets with the staff-parish relations committee once a year, without the pastor, to hear the committee's honest assessment of the pastor's performance. Members of the committee have "saved up" their concerns to report to the superintendent. They have not spoken directly with the pastor about their concerns because they "don't want to hurt the pastor's feelings." Following the meeting with the staff-parish relations committee, the superintendent meets with the pastor to share a summary of what the committee members said about his performance.

Scenario 2

The staff-parish relations committee meets once or twice a year to do an evaluation of the pastor's performance and to make a recommendation for pastoral compensation. Otherwise, the pastor and committee agree that there is no need to meet unless "there is a problem." Since there apparently have been no problems during the course of the year, the committee and pastor have not met together to reflect on their shared ministry or to give and receive feedback. The pastor is unpleasantly surprised by some of the negative comments in the committee's year-end evaluation.

Scenario 3

The staff-parish relations committee does not consider it appropriate for laypersons to evaluate the pastor's ministry performance. While no formal evaluation occurs, evaluation happens informally and indirectly in the parking lot. The concerns raised in these informal conversations are never addressed with the pastor. The congregation becomes divided between those who support the pastor and those who do not.

Scenario 4

A pastor is appointed to the church in response to the church's expressed need to focus on evangelism and church growth. This need is reaffirmed at the introductory meeting at the time of the appointment. For the first two years in the new appointment, the pastor invests a major portion of time to ministries focused on church growth. Neither the church's mission nor the pastor's goals are reviewed during this two-year period. There is growing discontent among some members, who feel that the pastor is neglecting care of persons whose ability to leave home is limited. This concern is conveyed to a member of the staff-parish relations committee, but it is never discussed directly with the pastor until the time of the evaluation.

Scenario 5

The pastor has been in ministry for twenty years. The chair of the staff-parish relations committee calls the pastor to set a date for the committee and pastor to meet in order to begin the evaluation process. The pastor tells the chairperson that there is no need for the committee to be involved in this process, noting, "This is a concern that the district superintendent and I will address."

Scenario 6

The staff-parish relations committee and the pastor get off to a good start in the new appointment. The church has completed a demographics study of the community, adopted vision and mission statements, and established clear goals. These are discussed with the pastor, who affirms the direction of the church and expresses enthusiasm for being a partner in ministry with this extraordinary congregation. There is great excitement in the first year of the appointment. However, as time passes, key lay leaders begin to notice that the pastor is not communicating and is not following through on commitments. When approached by the chairperson of the staff-parish relations committee, who is concerned about the pastor and the ministries of the church, the pastor admits to being "a little bit behind." However, she assures the chairperson that this is a temporary problem and that "there is nothing to worry about." More time passes, with no improvement. During the annual evaluation, the committee members give their feedback regarding unmet goals. The pastor becomes defensive and denies having agreed to anything that the committee identified as "unmet goals."

Scenario 7

A pastor of a racial-ethnic background different from the majority of the congregation is appointed; but there is no intentional preparation, no sharing and testing of assumptions. Neither are there deliberate opportunities for learning about cultural and racial differences among the covenant partners. The pastor and the members of the staff-parish relations committee proceed with an evaluation process, without inquiring and clarifying their understandings and expectations. Conflict and alienation take over where exciting, new possibilities for growth, learning, and witnessing might have been possible.

Reflect

Write a scenario from your own experience of ministry assessment.

> What is common to your experience and the scenarios above?

> What observations do you have about the process and the relationships described in each of these scenarios?

> Are there insights from your reflection on the seven
scenarios that shed light on the gaps and strengths of
the scenario you described?

These scenarios point out the complexity of the accountability and support issues that individuals and congregations face. In some of these cases, persons were invested in the ministries of the church, recognized that accountability was necessary, and made an attempt to carry out what they understood to be their responsibilities. In most situations the parties appeared to have had good intentions for the pastor and the church. In two instances (Scenario 3, by the committee, and Scenario 5, by the pastor), there were evasive actions. It is possible that fear of the process, a lack of clarity about roles and authority, or a lack of trust may have gotten in the way.

In each of these scenarios, it seems clear that *something* important was compromised; and the mission of the church and the ministry of the pastor were undermined in some way. Those involved may not have known precisely what went wrong; they knew only that what was done did not achieve the desired outcomes.

Many who have responsibilities in ministry assessment feel caught between extremes of overstepping their authority or abdicating their authority altogether, of over-functioning or under-functioning, of "telling it like it is" or keeping quiet. Nurture and accountability are understood as polar opposites, rather than as two aspects of support. This trap prevents laity and clergy from engaging in a mutual ministry that would benefit both the pastor and the mission of the church. It reflects an either/or way of seeing, a dualistic worldview that suppresses new possibilities for thinking and acting.

Weak systems of support and accountability give rise to problems and confusion. In the absence of mutually agreed-upon guidelines and processes for ministry assessment, potentially harmful forms of evaluation take over. The result is misunderstandings, conflicts, and divisions that are damaging to the community life and the mission of the church. Consequently, crucial ministries never get done. Faulty assumptions about the purpose of ministry assessment, poor processes, and lack of training for those who implement the assessment process contribute to resistance to evaluation and weaken the ministry of pastors and congregations.

Much is at stake in addressing these concerns. Ensuring the integrity of the church's ministry and the health of pastors will require that leaders at all levels of the church learn new ways to think about, approach, and practice the ministry of ministry assessment. Leaving ministry assessment to chance or employing models that are not grounded in biblical theology will, at best, contribute little to the witness of the church or, at worst, damage individuals and congregations. A plan agreed upon by all parties allows everyone to reflect and to learn from one another.

The model of ministry assessment proposed in this book is not offered as a solution to all of the church's problems. Neither does it provide a magic formula that guarantees happy outcomes, nor does it propose a quick fix. Indeed, this model is not at all about solutions, outcomes, or quick fixes. Such ends would not be desirable even if they were possible.

The process of ministry assessment described in these pages seeks to support mutual ministry and growth that is expressed in concrete acts of love. It is about growth in vocational competence and about assisting one another in bearing the fruits of faith. It provides a way through the joys and struggles that are sure to come when persons engage in shared ministry. It is offered as "a means of grace," a discipline through which the love of God can be mediated as we "watch over one another in love."[3] It is built on mutual trust and responsibility and lived out through covenantal relationships.

This book is a summons to pastors, laypersons, and district superintendents to imagine new possibilities for engaging in mutual ministry. It asks church leaders at all levels to consider, "What if . . . ?"

- What if accountability in ministry performance were covenantal and experienced as a gift?
- What if those who provided feedback saw themselves as companions in ministry and not simply as observers?
- What if growth in self-awareness, ministering competence, theological understanding, and Christian commitment[4] were the fruits of mutual engagement in ministry assessment?
- What if ministry assessment were built upon mutual trust and covenant-making?
- What if the process of ministry assessment were understood as a way of watching over one another in love and experienced as a means of grace?
- What if intentional ministry assessment required that the process of evaluation also be subject to review, critique, and revision?

The challenge and the opportunity are ours. There *is* a way. It *is* possible to involve pastors and laity in a process that creates an environment where mutual support and accountability are experienced as gifts that enhance the growth and ministry competence of both the pastor and the congregation. Pastors, congregations, and district superintendents can participate in a process of ongoing reflection and assessment that mediates grace and holds persons accountable for fruit-bearing faith. They can engage in ministry assessment that is *itself* ministry. There is a way to offer support without fostering moral weakness and to hold persons accountable without inflicting cruelty.

This book assists church leaders in creating a covenant-based ministry assessment process that promotes and holds together support and accountability and that contributes to the experience of ministry assessment as edifying for the church and the pastor or staff person. It presents a process that is congruent with a Wesleyan theology of grace and responsibility.

For the sake of clarity and coherence, I describe the covenantal ministry assessment process for a local church setting with the pastor, the staff-parish relations committee, and the district superintendent as the covenant partners. However, the process and practices can be adapted for use with other clergy and staff in a variety of ministry settings.

I use the term *ministry assessment* to describe a whole process, including the establishment of a covenant, periodic feedback, formalization of feedback, critique of the process, and covenant renewal. The terms *evaluation* and *formalization of feedback*, which refer to one part of the ministry assessment process, will be used interchangeably.

The first chapter considers emphases in Wesleyan theology that provide the theological groundwork for understanding ministry assessment as a process of growth in grace. It offers a basis for understanding ministry assessment and evaluation as a means by which persons of faith hold one another accountable for personal and social holiness.

Chapter 2 discusses *covenant* as the instrument for developing relationships and structures that support growth in ministry. It addresses questions such as these: What is a covenant? How does it function? Who are the covenant partners, and what are their roles? What does a covenant accomplish? This chapter also considers the importance of reflection and feedback in covenantal relationships.

Chapter 3 presents the steps in the process of ministry assessment and evaluation. These steps assist the covenant partners in conducting an evaluation as part of an ongoing process of mutual ministry consistent with Wesleyan theology. The first three steps are "Know the Context of Ministry," "Establish a Ministry Covenant," and "Give and Receive Regular Feedback." These steps provide the basis for the fourth step, "Formalize Feedback Through Evaluation."

The Appendices section contains sample forms and other materials to assist staff-parish relations committees in conducting a ministry assessment process that supports growth and requires accountability. These materials are meant to serve as a guide. They may be adapted to serve the particular needs of local churches or other ministry settings.

Notes

1. *The Book of Discipline of The United Methodist Church—2008* (Nashville: The United Methodist Publishing House, 2008), ¶101, p. 49.
2. Kenneth Pohly, "The Purpose and Function of Supervision in Ministry" (paper presented to the D.Min. Intensive Seminar, United Theological Society, Dayton, Ohio, February 12, 1981; revised 2004), pp. 1–2.
3. John Wesley, "The Nature, Design, and General Rules of the United Societies," in *The Works of John Wesley*, ed. Rupert E. Davies (Nashville: Abingdon, 1989), 9:69.
4. Kenneth Pohly, *Transforming the Rough Places: The Ministry of Supervision* (Franklin, TN: Providence House Publishers, 2001), pp. 107–08.

CHAPTER 1

Theological Foundations

**"The coherence of faith with ministries of love
forms the discipline of Wesleyan spirituality
and Christian discipleship."[1]**

The decision to make theology the starting point for presenting this model of ministry assessment is intentional. First, an essential task of the church is the articulation of what it believes, what it seeks to embody, and what it wants to communicate through its life and witness. Without a clear theology, the church is at risk of being "tossed to and fro and blown about by every wind of doctrine." (Eph. 4:14) Theological reflection establishes the purpose and provides a rudder for the ministry of evaluation. It engages disciples in asking the question, "What does God have to do with this?"

Second, this book is based upon the assumption that *ministry assessment is itself a ministry*. It is not simply a way of getting ministry done or a means to an end. It is *a way of doing ministry*[2] or, to use Wesley's words, a way of "watch[ing] over one another in love"[3] in order that we may grow in holiness.

1

As such, the task of ministry assessment is fundamentally a theological task.

Third, theological reflection as the starting point in considering ministry assessment acknowledges and reminds us that we are ultimately accountable to God. Like everything else we do as Christians, the ministry assessment process must be examined in light of what we understand to be God's will for the church in the world.

The Book of Discipline of The United Methodist Church spells out the critical nature of our theological task and exhorts us "to test various expressions of faith by asking: 'Are they true? Appropriate? Clear? Cogent? Credible? Are they based on love? Do they provide the Church and its members with a witness that is faithful to the gospel?'"[4] These questions apply to the *ministries* that are carried out on behalf of the church, the *processes* by which we evaluate the effectiveness of these ministries, and the quality of the *relationships* that exist among those who are part of the process.

Reflect

What do the processes and relationships that are integral to ministry assessment and evaluation in your congregation reflect about your individual and collective understanding of God, the nature of ministry, and discipleship? One way to engage this question is to imagine a third party making a list of what he or she understands to be your congregation's beliefs, based solely on observing your ministry assessment process. What would the list contain?

> Would it reflect your beliefs about God, the church, and ministry?

> Would it affirm or challenge your beliefs?

> Would it cause you to change the way you carry out the ministry assessment process? If so, what would change?

Beliefs about God, the church, and the nature of ministry are *implied* in the way we practice ministry. Through regular, critical reflection and self-examination, we can discern more clearly wherein we need to change either our practice or our beliefs with regard to ministry assessment and evaluation.

A starting point for articulating a theology for ministry assessment and evaluation would be to explore the Scriptures: What basis for ministry assessment do you find in Scripture? What does Scripture suggest about the form it should take? For example, what do texts such as Jeremiah 31:31-32, John 15:12-17, 1 Corinthians 12, 2 Corinthians 3:1-6, Ephesians 4:1-16, and 1 Peter 2:4 say to us about covenant, love for one another, the variety of gifts within the body of Christ, and the equipping of the saints for the work of ministry? Although I will not expand upon these texts here, those who engage in the process of ministry assessment recommended in this book are encouraged to reflect on these and other Scripture passages as a means of articulating a theology of ministry assessment and evaluation.

Reflect

> Spend some time alone reflecting on two or three of the Scripture passages above. If a good Bible commentary is available, consult it to help interpret the meaning of the passages.

> Discuss your thoughts with a small group of persons who have done the same thing.

> How do these passages inform our understanding and practice of ministry assessment?

In the pages that follow, I explore emphases in Wesleyan theology as a way of grounding the practice of ministry assessment in God's purposes. It is fair to ask, "Why Wesley?" Examining the connections between Wesley's theology and the process of ministry assessment makes two things possible. First, identifying these connections allows us to reconsider our common roots as United Methodists and their implications for the way we live out our lives in Christian community. It answers the question, "Why is it particularly fitting for United Methodists to follow this process?"

The second reason to look at Wesley is purely practical. Confining our reflections to Wesley's theological emphases is more manageable in a text of this size. The focus on Wesley is by no means intended to discount or diminish the biblical and theological beliefs that we share with all Christians. Rather, it is to consider one way of appropriating those beliefs in our practice of ministry and, more specifically, in our practice of ministry assessment and evaluation.

The ministry assessment process I propose is consistent with Wesley's understanding of God's grace, the life of holiness, the means of grace, and mutual support and accountability. Let us look briefly at these emphases in Wesley's theology that find expression in the model of ministry assessment and evaluation that follows.

SALVATION BY GRACE IS A GRADUAL PROCESS

The story of salvation is first of all a story about *God's grace*— forgiving, restoring, and empowering us for growth in love. The story of salvation is also a story about *our response*—about receiving the gift of God's grace and living a life of holiness. Wesley spoke about salvation as a process of transformation brought about through God's prevenient, justifying, and sanctifying grace. *The Book of Discipline* describes the Wesleyan understanding of grace this way:

Grace pervades our understanding of Christian faith and life. By grace we mean the undeserved, unmerited, and loving action of God in human existence through the ever-present Holy Spirit. While the grace of God is undivided, it precedes salvation as "prevenient grace," continues in "justifying grace," and is brought to fruition in "sanctifying grace."[5]

God seeks us before we seek God. Before we are even aware, God's love surrounds us and reaches out to us. This *prevenient* (before-our-knowing) grace is given entirely at God's initiative. We do not earn it; we *cannot* earn it. God, who loves us beyond comprehension, gives grace freely and completely. Prevenient grace awakens our senses and deepens our desire for God. *Justifying* grace forgives us and overcomes our guilt and alienation from God. It sets us free and opens the possibility of new life. It brings about a "change in how we view ourselves, others, and the world around us."[6] *Sanctifying* grace, the third way grace is operative in the believer's life, is a process of growing and maturing in holiness, of being transformed into the likeness of Christ and "perfected" in love.

This progressive movement of grace has been described in this way: "God not only justifies, thereby providing the foundation for the new life, but opens up hitherto unimaginable possibilities for *growth* in grace. God's goal is to *create us anew, to transform us, to restore us to health and to our role as the image of God*."[7] Bishop Kenneth Carder comments, "For United Methodists, the Christian life is an ongoing, dynamic pilgrimage toward total restoration of the divine image. It is the endless journey into holiness or perfect love."[8]

We are surrounded by grace, we are saved by grace, and we grow by grace. Our self-understanding, our relationship with our neighbor, and our understanding of God's transforming action at work in us and all creation are defined by God's gift of grace and our appropriation of this gift in our lives.

Faith and Fruit Go Together

The experience of God's saving grace results in a life of holy living, a life in which the believer grows into the likeness of Christ. In other words, *faith is inherently fruit bearing*. According to Wesley, a lively faith is "fruitful in bringing forth good works." True faith is expressed in love of God and neighbor.

> As strongly as [Wesley] stressed faith as the foundation of the Christian life, he was equally intent upon love as the fruition of that life. Faith is not an end in itself, but rather a necessary means. Faith is in order to love. . . . The genius of the gospel, in [Wesley's] eyes, is its power to generate a faith that impels the believer to the quality of love that *works* for righteousness.[9]

For Wesley, faith and works are inseparably connected. Love of God is expressed concretely in love of neighbor. We are justified by faith; and the fruit of faith is good works. Faithfulness is not merely giving assent to a set of doctrines or beliefs. For Wesley, salvation involves transformation that leads to outward expressions of love. It is not possible to have the love of Jesus merely in our hearts. A prominent aspect of Wesley's thought is that "love must be *active*; it is something which is done. There can be no 'inward' love without a corresponding change in one's active relationship with God and neighbor."[10] The love of Jesus Christ transforms us, and the effect is an increase in the love of God and neighbor.

The necessary relationship—and tension—between grace and good works was something that Wesley was continuously called upon to defend. His insistence that faith produced good works set him apart from some of his contemporaries. Yet he held to this belief, and it became a hallmark of Methodism. This foundational belief is reflected in the Articles of Religion of

The Methodist Church and the Confession of Faith of The Evangelical United Brethren Church:

Article X—Of Good Works

Although good works, which are the fruits of faith, and follow after justification, cannot put away our sins, and endure the severity of God's judgment; yet are they pleasing and acceptable to God in Christ, and spring out of a true and lively faith, insomuch that by them a lively faith may be as evidently known as a tree is discerned by its fruit.[11]

Article X—Good Works

We believe good works are the necessary fruits of faith and follow regeneration but they do not have the virtue to remove our sins or to avert divine judgment. We believe good works, pleasing and acceptable to God in Christ, spring from a true and living faith, for through and by them faith is made evident.[12]

It is clear that for early Methodists personal and social holiness, inner assurance of God's grace and outward acts of love toward neighbor, and works of piety and works of mercy are held together in unity. They do not exist apart from one another.

THE MEANS OF GRACE SUPPORT GROWTH IN LOVE

Wesley believed that growth in love was nurtured through participation in the means of grace. In *Responsible Grace: John Wesley's Practical Theology*, United Methodist theologian Randy Maddox points to the role of the means of grace in nurturing persons in the way of salvation:

Wesley considered present human salvation to be fundamentally a gradual therapeutic process that grows out of our responsive participation in God's forgiving and empowering grace. In its most normative sense, salvation appears neither unilaterally nor spontaneously in our lives; it must be progressively empowered and responsibly nurtured along the Way of Salvation. This point leads directly into Wesley's understanding of the "means of grace."[13]

Methodists were expected to "evidence their desire of salvation" by "doing no harm," by "doing good," and by "attending upon all the ordinances of God."[14] Wesley formed societies and classes in which members met in order "to pray together, to receive the word of exhortation, and to watch over one another in love, that they may help each other to work out their salvation."[15]

The means of grace—including prayer, searching of the Scriptures, the Lord's Supper, fasting, Christian fellowship, and holy conferencing—were considered essential to holy living. Salvation was to be worked out in Christian community through mutual support and accountability.

> *Christian discipleship requires being held in love and being held accountable.* We simply cannot follow Christ apart from a community that holds us in compassion and calls us to accountability. Solitary discipleship is a misnomer. We cannot be Christian alone. Only with the support, corrections, and help of other disciples can we follow Christ. . . . Christian discipleship is a journey toward maturity in Christ, requiring a lifetime of discipline and accountability.[16]

While all of the means of grace contribute to persons' growth in love, "conferring together," or "conferencing," has particular relevance to the matter of support and accountability that are integral to the model of ministry assessment presented in this book.

Conferring together was . . . a means by which . . . lay communities of faith could "try the spirits [to see] whether they are of God" (1 John 4:1). By comparing one's own experiences with those of other members of the community and with Scripture, one could determine whether one's point of view and understanding was consistent with the Scriptures, "the church of the ages," and fellow believers. Wesley frequently advised persons to measure their own experience and interpretation against that of the community. . . . "[C]onference" serves not only this corrective and restrictive function, but also the positive and catalytic function of a means of grace when, through consultation and conversation, the Spirit is able to convict, convince, and open up new possibilities for understanding and growth.[17]

IMPLICATIONS FOR MINISTRY ASSESSMENT

Reflect

Take time to think about the questions below. Then discuss your responses with others before reading the following list of possible implications:

> What do God's unmerited grace, faith expressed in good works, and the means of grace have to do with the assessment of effectiveness in ministry?

> How do these hallmarks of Wesley's theology relate to our current practices of ministry assessment?

> What would a ministry assessment process based upon these theological assumptions look like?

> What characteristics would describe the relationships in such a process?

- A ministry assessment process rooted in Wesleyan theology would be *grace-filled*. The persons involved would show genuine care and concern for one another. They would support one another and hold one another accountable for their commitments. They would not judge one another's worth. They would assume that God is active and present in the process, extending grace to all and transforming individuals and the community through the process. Relationships of accountability and support would be extended and embraced as a gift.
- A model of ministry assessment coherent with Wesley's theology would be built on *covenantal relationships* and *disciplines*. These relationships and disciplines would be intentionally established and maintained for the purpose of creating and supporting an environment conducive to honest sharing of feedback and to increasing in vocational competence.
- The ministry assessment process would assist persons in reflecting on the congruence (or incongruence) between their beliefs and their practice, provide feedback in a manner that encourages and supports learning from experience, extend care to persons as they gain new insights from failures, and celebrate growth.
- A ministry assessment process based on Wesley's theology would hold persons accountable for demonstrating *fruits* and keeping commitments made in covenant with the community of faith. Mutually established commitments would provide the basis for assessing effectiveness.
- Those entrusted with the responsibility for evaluating another's ministry would understand their roles and responsibilities as a sacred call to ministry. They would

engage in self-examination of their own faithfulness in keeping with their covenant commitments.

- Disagreements, grievances, and conflicts would be worked out through mutually agreed-upon processes and covenants.
- Ministry assessment would be a communal endeavor, involving partners in ministry, each with a different role but no one subservient to the other. Members of staff-parish relations committees would be considered companions in ministry, not simply observers. Mutual trust would be nurtured among the members of the community.

These are some of the implications for ministry assessment and evaluation that could be drawn from Scripture and Wesleyan theology. Readers are encouraged to discuss and to expand upon this list.

It seems safe to assert that Wesley (1) affirmed the need for accountability in discipleship; (2) had a method for supporting it; (3) and held fast to the belief that accountability was nurtured in the community of believers. In his sermon "Catholic Spirit," Wesley said:

> First, love me. . . . "If thine heart be right, as mine with thy heart," then love me with a very tender affection. . . . [S]econdly, commend me to God in all thy prayers; wrestle with him in my behalf, that he would speedily correct what he sees amiss, and supply what is wanting in me. . . . [T]hirdly, provoke me to love and to good works. . . . Oh speak . . . and conduce, either to the amending of my faults, the strengthening of my weaknesses, the building me up in love, or the making me more fit in any kind for the Master's use.[18]

According to Wesley's approach, the steps in accountability and support are to love me, pray for me, evaluate me, and assist me in my growth[19] for the sake of Christ and the gospel. Wesley's words express a deep yearning within the church today. The extent to which the church is able to engage in this kind of mutual support and accountability in ministry will determine greatly its effectiveness in bearing witness to the gospel of Christ.

In the next chapter, we explore the use of covenant as the means for holding together support and accountability in ministry assessment. We consider what a covenant is, what it does, how it is nurtured, and what difference it makes for those who are evaluated and those who are evaluators.

Notes

1. *The Book of Discipline of The United Methodist Church—2008* (Nashville: The United Methodist Publishing House, 2008), ¶101, p. 48.
2. Kenneth Pohly, *Transforming the Rough Places: The Ministry of Supervision* (Franklin, TN: Providence House Publishers, 2001), p. 108.
3. John Wesley, "The Nature, Design, and General Rules of the United Societies," in *The Works of John Wesley*, ed. Rupert E. Davies (Nashville: Abingdon, 1989), 9:69.
4. *Book of Discipline*, ¶104, p. 75.
5. Ibid., ¶101, pp. 45–46.
6. Kenneth Carder, *Living Our Beliefs: The United Methodist Way* (Nashville: Discipleship Resources, 1998), p. 62.
7. Theodore Runyon, *The New Creation: John Wesley's Theology Today* (Nashville: Abingdon Press, 1998), pp. 83–84.
8. Carder, *Living Our Beliefs*, pp. 71–72.
9. Albert Outler, ed., *John Wesley* (New York: Oxford University Press, 1964), p. 221.

10. Henry H. Knight III, *The Presence of God in the Christian Life: John Wesley and the Means of Grace* (Metuchen, NJ: Scarecrow Press, 1992), p. 4.
11. *Book of Discipline*, ¶103, pp. 61–62.
12. Ibid., ¶103, p. 69.
13. Randy L. Maddox, *Responsible Grace: John Wesley's Practical Theology* (Nashville: Kingswood Books, 1994), p. 192.
14. *Book of Discipline*, ¶103, pp. 73–74.
15. Ibid., ¶103, pp. 72.
16. Carder, *Living Our Beliefs*, pp. 76, 77.
17. Runyon, *The New Creation*, p. 127.
18. John Wesley, "Catholic Spirit," in *John Wesley's Sermons: An Anthology*, ed. Albert C. Outler and Richard P. Heitzenrater (Nashville: Abingdon Press, 1991), pp. 306–07.
19. Richard Yeager, ed., *Developing and Evaluating an Effective Ministry: A Manual for Pastors and Diaconal Ministers* (Nashville: General Board of Higher Education and Ministry, n.d.), p. 1.

CHAPTER 2

Holding Support and Accountability Together

"The ministry of all Christians consists
of privilege and obligation. The privilege
is a relationship with God that is deeply
spiritual. The obligation is to respond to God's
call to holy living in the world. In the
United Methodist tradition these two
dimensions of Christian discipleship are
wholly interdependent."[1]

The assertion that Christian discipleship consists of the
privilege of a *relationship* with God and the obligation
to *respond* to God's call through holy living is central to
Wesleyan theology. This assertion gives rise to an important
question: How can these two interdependent dimensions
be held together? My proposal is that a covenant makes
this possible.

15

The process of ministry assessment described in this book assumes that holding together faith and action, theology and practice, support and accountability, personal and social holiness is essential for faithfulness. It proposes further that it is the practices of covenant-making and covenant-keeping that make it possible to hold these dimensions together.

The notion of covenant supports and enlivens Wesley's understanding that we are saved by grace, that faith is expressed and evidenced in fruit, and that we can avail ourselves of God's grace through practices that make us more open to receiving this gift. A covenant is God's act of inviting us into a grace-filled and life-giving relationship in which we are continually being transformed by the love of God. A covenant is a sign of our acceptance of the grace of God. It is an expression of our desire and intention to be accountable to God and to one another for living a life of personal and social holiness. A covenant is a channel of God's love—a means of grace—because it establishes the relationships and sets the conditions that keep us attentive to the Spirit, who is always present.

Thus, covenant-making and covenant-keeping are at the heart of the ministry assessment process in this book. For this reason, in this chapter we examine what a covenant is and how it functions in ministry assessment and evaluation.

What Is a Covenant?

A covenant is a mutually created commitment to ministry. It is grounded in our relationship with God, who created us and called us to ministry. It is a statement of intention, usually written, that binds the parties in a mutually agreed-upon process to see that particular segments of ministry are done and reflected on. A covenant is Spirit directed and grounded in our relationship with God. It says, "Here is what we will endeavor to do together and how we will hold one another accountable." It is a commitment to life and growth.[2]

Kenneth Pohly helpfully distinguishes between a contract and a covenant. He characterizes the customary contract this way:

> The traditional way of making an agreement between an employee and the institution for which that person works is for the institution to offer a standard contract, which is used for everyone and written without reference to any particular person, spelling out the conditions within which the employees will work. The institution sets the conditions. The employee may or may not be given an opportunity to modify the contract. Generally, however, the employer sets the parameters and the employee signs the contract, which then becomes a legal document.[3]

Pohly points out that our Hebrew-Christian heritage offers covenant-making as a more collaborative way of making an agreement. In this arrangement all the participating partners help set the conditions. The covenant is mutually negotiated and mutually binding. It is a commitment to ministry and growth rather than an externally imposed requirement of employment. A covenant is flexible and can be revised by the covenant partners as needs and conditions change. In the covenantal relationship, the persons *and* the ministries they perform are cared for with great intent.[4]

WHAT DOES A COVENANT DO?

A covenant changes the way the conditions and expectations are set for ministry. But that is only the beginning. A covenant also changes the dynamics of ministry—the way we approach our work, carry out our commitments, relate to others, and think about ministry assessment. A covenantal approach subtly yet decidedly shifts the goal of ministry assessment and evaluation from *judging* and *correcting* to *growing* and *learning*—and that shift sets something new in motion.

Reflect

How, do you think, does a covenant create this change in goal? Discuss your responses with others, and then consider the following points:

- A covenant communicates that *the business of "being the church" is too important to leave to chance*. It assumes that growth, faithfulness, and competence do not happen automatically or accidentally. Rather, they are brought about through careful examination of our practice in light of the gospel of Christ and through deliberate disciplines that help us listen and learn in Christian community. The covenant is the church's way of saying, "We will not just sit back and hope for the best. We will intentionally create the environment and establish the conditions for growth to happen. We will take the initiative and the responsibility to be a community of formation in which we commit to live out our faith through specific actions, engage in self-examination, and present ourselves to the covenantal community in order to grow in our love of God and our neighbor."
- A covenant communicates *our intent to care for one another*. It acknowledges that we all need to be supported and nurtured as we seek to be faithful to the ministries to which we have been called and sent; and it demonstrates our commitment to one another's growth.
- A covenant holds us *mutually accountable for the commitments we make to God and to one another*. It establishes joint ownership for those commitments "so that whatever is 'out

there' . . . can no longer be ignored or relegated to the irrelevant because it has become integral to the personal or corporate self."[5]

- A covenant sets *priorities, establishes structures, provides boundaries, and identifies procedures around which ministry can occur and be evaluated.*[6] It establishes goals for the use of time and resources. It makes provisions for reflection on experiences in ministry and for sharing of feedback. It states agreed-upon procedures and expectations that will guide the process of giving and receiving feedback. It makes clear mutually agreed-upon plans and intentions.

- A covenant saves *persons from the isolation that undermines support and accountability in ministry.* It binds us to this community for our own sake and for the sake of the gospel. A covenant says, "Christian life and ministry is a journey in community. We cannot go it alone."

- A covenant is a *vehicle for assessing effectiveness in ministry in a collaborative and open way.* We are all familiar with the kinds of evaluations that are done in the parking lot. (We may have participated in some of these ourselves!) In a paper entitled "Theological and Theoretical Foundations for Evaluating Ministry," Richard Yeager refers to these parking-lot evaluations as "covert evaluation" and points to the demonic and destructive results of doing evaluation outside the circle of grace.[7] A covenant provides a way to build trust among group members and to restore trust when it has been broken. It also creates an environment in which persons can "speak the truth in love."

- A covenant nurtures and enables *learning and growth.* It assumes that growth and effectiveness are the purpose of ministry assessment. It creates conditions in which growth can occur and pays attention to what is needed to nurture it. A covenantal approach monitors and celebrates progress and provides a means by which it can be measured. It identifies those things that have contributed to or stifled growth, and it makes changes to enhance future learning.

WHO ARE THE PARTNERS IN THE COVENANT?

By definition a covenant involves more than one partner. A covenant does not exist without partnerships, nor can it be fulfilled without multiple partners and processes working together. The partners will vary from one ministry setting to another; but, regardless of the setting, a covenant-based ministry assessment process assumes that each of these partners has an essential role to play. Each has a different function, but no one is more important than another. The process is dependent upon each one understanding his or her role and claiming his or her authority and responsibility for carrying it out. Together these partners work toward a common purpose of growing in faithful and competent practice of ministry.

The Book of Discipline identifies three partners in the process of evaluation for full members and local pastors serving as pastors of local churches: the *district superintendent*, the *staff-parish relations committee*, and *the pastor*.

> The district superintendent, in consultation with the pastor-parish relations committee, will evaluate annually the pastors' effectiveness for ministry (¶¶334.2c, 421, 635.2n, q), using criteria, processes, and training developed by the cabinet and the Board of Ordained Ministry. The pastors in the local churches shall participate annually in an evaluation with the committee on pastor-parish relations for use in an ongoing effective ministry and for identifying continuing education needs and plans (¶258.2g[5]), using criteria, processes and training developed by the Board of Ordained Ministry and the cabinet.[8]

What Gives Life to the Covenant?

Two essential dynamics give life, energy, and meaning to the covenant: *reflection* and *feedback*. These dynamics engage the covenant partners in an intentional process of looking at their life and actions in light of their understanding of God's presence and purposes and of assisting one another in acting out of God's new revelation. "The Christian life is a growing thing and to grow we need to look at ourselves to understand what is causing us to grow or not grow."[9] Pausing to reflect on our practice of ministry enables us to look at and learn from our actions. Receiving feedback enables us to know how others experience our leadership. Without reflection and feedback it is much harder to see or to learn from our experience.

Reflection

In a chapter entitled "Why Smart Organizations Don't Learn," in the book *Learning Organizations: Developing Cultures for Tomorrow's Workplace*, Lisa Marshall, Sandra Mobley, and Gene Calvert have the following to say about action, reflection, and learning:

> This is a process that says that learning doesn't stop when action is taken. Rather, that's when learning begins. When we reflect on the action, we come to better understanding about what happened, what worked or didn't and how we should act in the future. By building in pauses to reflect and digest, participants draw on their real-world experiences as the primary source of their learning.[10]

A covenant holds together support and accountability by making provisions for the partners to pause and to reflect on their actions and how these actions fit into God's transforming work in the world. Reflection on our experience is the way we participate in and contribute toward our own growth and the growth of others.

In *Putting It Together in the Parish,* James D. Glasse identifies three steps in a reflective process. (His comments apply equally to laity.)

> The first step is *respect*. Most pastors object when I say: "You do not respect your work." But most parish ministers I know just do *not* "respect" their work. In the literal meaning of the word, they do not look back on their actions. That's what the word means: "to respect, to look again." A pastor who does not look back regularly at what he [or she] is doing, does not respect his [or her] work.
>
> The second step is *regard.* This means: "To keep in view, to look closely, to hold in high esteem."
>
> The third step is *recognition*, literally: "to know again, to perceive a thing as previously known."[11]

Reflection on one's ministry practice is for the purpose of learning from one's experience. It might be assumed that reflection on work is a common practice among Christians, most especially among pastors. This is not necessarily the case. It is all too easy to fall prey to the pressure to rush from one program or one appointment to the next, without pausing to reflect on what we have done and learned or considering what our busyness has to do with God's purposes. This concern underlines the importance of intentionally establishing relationships and structures to support and hold one another accountable in ministry.

Theological reflection is the way in which we think not only about our experience but also about how God is present in the events and interactions of our lives. The purpose of theological reflection is to deepen awareness of and correspondence between our beliefs and our action, see our ministries in the light of the gospel, make explicit the connections between our beliefs about God and our actions, open ourselves to what God wants to teach us, and deepen the conversation with other partners in the covenant.

Feedback

Sharing feedback might be considered a modern version of "holy conferencing." As pointed out in the previous chapter, Wesley considered this kind of conversation to be a means of grace. The purpose of sharing feedback sounds very much like Bishop Kenneth Carder's description of the role of Christian conference:

> Conversation with other Christians around issues of faith and mission is a means by which God guides and strengthens us. Sharing our understandings and struggles with others who are seeking to participate in God's life and work opens new avenues of divine grace and guidance. Through such sharing, the Holy Spirit is present to direct, empower, and transform. . . . In the midst of honest discussion and through the power of the Holy Spirit, the risen Christ comes to provide food for our journey toward the fulfillment of God's purpose.[12]

Or as Art Gafke puts the matter: "[F]eedback is a process of communicating directly to an individual what you experience, observe, think, and feel about his or her leadership. . . . A congregation's maturity of faith and practice of love can be measured by the way in which feedback is given and received."[13] I will say more in the next chapter about how feedback is given and received.

WHAT DIFFERENCE DOES A COVENANT MAKE?

In the preceding paragraphs, I described what a covenant is, what it does, and what gives it life. The question that remains is this: "So what? What difference does it make?" One of the ways to examine this question is to look again at the seven scenarios described in the Introduction (pp. vi-viii). What would have been different in these situations had a covenant for ministry been established?

Reflect

Consider the following scenarios describing what difference a covenant makes. Do you agree or disagree with my analysis? What would you add to the changes mentioned? Identify and discuss any issues that would not be addressed by the use of a covenant in developing and assessing effective ministry. Do you have other thoughts about what could strengthen the process? What resources are available?

Scenario 1

A covenant would have made provisions for regular meetings throughout the year in which the committee could have addressed their concerns directly to the pastor. It is likely that the pastor and committee together would have arrived at solutions by speaking openly, sharing information and insights, and drawing on their collective wisdom. They would not have had to wait for the district superintendent's visit to confront and address the issues. The district superintendent would not have been "triangled" into communicating the committee's concerns to the pastor for them.

Scenario 2

A covenant would assume that ministry assessment is an ongoing process rather than an annual event. The staff-parish relations committee and the pastor would have been meeting on a regular basis to check on progress on agreed-upon goals and would have addressed any areas of concern as they arose. The staff-parish relations committee would have had a much broader understanding of their role and responsibility as partners in ministry with the pastor. The process of ministry assessment would have culminated in a year-end evaluation, but the pastor would not have been surprised by the committee's year-end feedback.

Scenario 3

A covenant makes clear the expectations of the covenant partners. The members would have reviewed their responsibilities as outlined in *The Book of Discipline* in which the staff-parish relations committee's role is explicitly identified as one of the partners in this process. The committee would have availed itself of resources, including training offered by the district superintendent and/or the conference board of ordained ministry. There would have been clear expectations and processes for addressing concerns and these would have been clearly communicated to members of the congregation. Issues would have been addressed openly. Conflict would have been engaged in healthy ways, and the sharp division in the congregation could have been avoided.

Scenario 4

A covenant would have contained provision for regular consultation between the staff-parish relations committee and pastor regarding mutually agreed-upon goals. The plan would have been periodically reviewed, and revisions would have been made as needed. The congregation would have been clear about its mission and goals, and changing needs would have been discovered through the laity's reflection on its ministry. Structures and relationships would have been in place to enable the pastor and laity to discuss how they would meet this need for visitation of persons whose ability to leave home is limited. This might have been an opportunity for exploring creative possibilities for beginning a more intentional ministry to such persons, a ministry shared by the pastor and the laity.

Scenario 5

A covenant between the pastor and the staff-parish relations committee would have been established to include expectations and procedures for ministry assessment. There would have been joint ownership for the covenant, since all parties in the covenant would have understood and agreed upon the process. The district superintendent would have made his or her expectations regarding ministry assessment clear to both the pastor and the committee. The pastor would have understood the role of laity in ministry assessment and would not have been able to complete twenty years in parish ministry without participating with laity in this process. A covenant may have served to diminish the pastor's resistance and helped the pastor welcome ministry assessment with laypeople as an opportunity for growth through shared ministry.

Scenario 6

A covenant would have included a clear agreement about the pastor's plan for ministry. The plan would have included specific goals, and it would have described the actions and initiatives that would be taken by the pastor as well as the expected outcomes. (The congregation also would have had a similar statement of goals and commitments.) At the time of evaluation, the pastor and the committee would not have had different understandings about the commitments made. There would have been mutual accountability for commitments kept or not kept. The reasons for not fulfilling the commitments would have been addressed.

Scenario 7

In *Meeting God at the Boundaries: Cross-Cultural–Cross-Racial Clergy Appointments,* Lucia Ann McSpadden shares this observation of a clergyperson:

> When things are going well, race and culture do not enter into the situation strongly. However, when there is confusion and conflict, race and culture quickly drift to the top. The fact that these committees have not been proactive during "peaceful" times in fostering greater understanding of cultural/ethnic issues among committee members, in the congregation, and between the congregation and the pastor makes for a more volatile situation when confusion and/or crisis does develop.[14]

Ministry covenants in cross-cultural and cross-racial appointments provide an opportunity for pastors and committee members to be proactive in fostering greater understanding and appreciation for cultural and racial differences. Regular feedback sessions create an environment in which feelings can be expressed and issues addressed. District superintendents have a critical role to play in providing resources and support as covenant partners with pastors and staff-parish relations committee members.

In *Many Faces, One Church,* the authors note that the performance review of a racial-ethnic minority pastor in a cross-cultural–cross-racial appointment must aim to enhance the pastor's effectiveness and not focus on "how this stranger fits into the local church or community." The final goal of the review, the authors suggest, is to collaborate with and compliment the church and the pastor. This is not a time to point out deficits and weaknesses of the pastor or the church. The entire process should be a mutually agreed upon assessment of the pastor-church partnership. . . . If the process is to be truly beneficial, then the pastor must be given information about the criteria used for later evaluation.[15]

Adhering to such practices does not constitute special treatment. A mutually agreed-upon ministry covenant should be the standard for *all* persons in ministry. When such a process is not in place, persons in cross-racial and cross-cultural appointments are at higher risk of being undermined by stereotypes, false assumptions, and judgments based on incorrect or inadequate information and cultural bias.

DOES A COVENANT GUARANTEE SUCCESS?

A covenant does not eliminate the possibility of failure, nor does it guarantee success. A covenant may fail because it is inadequate, limited by our lack of vision, or impossible to fulfill. It may fail because one or more of the partners breaks the covenant. When these things occur, some may be tempted to resort to regulating ministry and ministers by creating rigid standards and policies,[16] fashioning one-size-fits-all approaches, or sitting back and "just letting it happen" in the hope that everything will turn out all right. These methods pose a much greater risk to individuals and to the witness of the church than does a covenant that is not fulfilled. While a covenant does not guarantee success, a process of ministry assessment and evaluation built upon covenant-making and covenant-keeping provides a means by which support and accountability can be held together in the practice of ministry. It provides a means by which ministry partners can reflect upon their purpose, celebrate their accomplishments, and learn from their failures as well as their successes.

Chapter 3 explores the practical application of Wesley's theology (the ongoing transformation of all creation through the grace of God; faith expressed in good works; accountability and support for Christian life and ministry through the means of grace) to the process of ministry assessment and evaluation. In that chapter, I describe how to implement a covenantal ministry assessment process, provide references to materials in the Appendices section for assistance in carrying out the process, and conclude with comments about training in the use of this model.

Notes

1. *The Book of Discipline of The United Methodist Church—2008* (Nashville: The United Methodist Publishing House, 2008), ¶134, pp. 91–92.
2. See Kenneth Pohly, *Transforming the Rough Places: The Ministry of Supervision* (Franklin, TN: Providence House Publishers, 2001), 141–44.
3. Kenneth Pohly, "An Evaluation Program Devoted to Wholeness for Persons and Institutions" (paper delivered at United Theological Seminary, Dayton, Ohio, March 2004), pp. 3–4.
4. Ibid., p. 4.
5. Pohly, *Transforming the Rough Places*, p. 88.
6. Ibid., p. 108.
7. Richard Yeager, "Theological and Theoretical Foundations for Evaluating Ministry" (Nashville: Division of Ordained Ministry, General Board of Higher Education and Ministry, The United Methodist Church, 1990), p. 8.
8. *Book of Discipline*, ¶350.1, p. 267.

9. Yeager, "Theological and Theoretical Foundations for Evaluating Ministry," p. 4.

10. Lisa J. Marshall, Sandy Mobley, and Gene Calvert, "Why Smart Organizations Don't Learn," in *Learning Organizations: Developing Cultures for Tomorrow's Workplace*, ed. Sarita Chawla and John Renesch (Portland, OR: Productivity Press, 1995), p. 122.

11. James D. Glasse, *Putting It Together in the Parish* (Nashville: Abingdon Press, 1972), p. 72.

12. Kenneth Carder, *Living Our Beliefs: The United Methodist Way* (Nashville: Discipleship Resources, 1998), p. 90.

13. Art Gafke, *Assessment: Giving and Receiving Feedback. Ministry Assessment Process* (Nashville: General Board of Higher Education and Ministry, The United Methodist Church, n.d.), p. 4.

14. Lucia Ann McSpadden, *Meeting God at the Boundaries: Cross-Cultural–Cross-Racial Clergy Appointments* (Nashville: General Board of Higher Education and Ministry, The United Methodist Church, 2003), p. 107.

15. Ernest S. Lyght, Glory E. Dharmaraj, and Jacob S. Dharmaraj, *Many Faces, One Church: A Manual for Cross-Racial and Cross-Cultural Ministry* (Nashville: Abingdon Press, 2006), p. 66.

16. Pohly, *Transforming the Rough Places*, p. 144.

CHAPTER 3

Steps in the
Ministry Assessment Process

"Our theological task is essentially practical.
**It informs the individual's daily decisions
and serves the Church's life and work. While highly
theoretical constructions of Christian thought
make important contributions to theological
understanding, we finally measure the truth of such
statements in relation to their practical significance.
Our interest is to incorporate the promises and
demands of the gospel into our daily lives."**[1]

If we believe that God's grace is freely given, that transformation through growth in grace is an ongoing process, that covenantal relationships support learning and growth, and that faith is expressed in concrete acts of love, then how will we go about the process of assessment and evaluation of ministry? Are there specific practices and steps that will express and bear witness to our beliefs about God, the mission of the church, and our life together as Christian disciples? How can we implement and practice ministry assessment and evaluation in a way that is congruent with Wesleyan theology?

The steps that follow are an attempt to provide a ministry assessment process that embodies the beliefs that are at the heart of Wesleyan theology. It proposes a means by which support and accountability can be held together in covenant in ministry assessment. It offers a way for the church to lovingly and deliberately address the common concerns related to ministry performance that have been sources of confusion, pain, and mistrust to the detriment of the church's life and witness (such as those described in the scenarios in the Introduction).

STEP 1: KNOW THE CONTEXT OF MINISTRY.

Ministry is not generic. It is defined according to specific times, places, and needs. That Jesus was well aware of the context for his ministry is evidenced throughout the Gospels. His ministry of healing, forgiving, and preaching was specific to the needs of persons and communities. He knew those with whom he spoke and ate. He knew who opposed him and when he was in dangerous territory. He knew who held power and who was disenfranchised. He was cognizant of the religious and political factions of his day. His preaching and teaching were contextual; his ministry was expressed in the particular. Although his mission was universal and timeless, his ministry consisted of specific acts of love.

We too must know our context for ministry. A meaningful ministry covenant cannot be created in a vacuum. In the previous chapter, I set forth the importance of a covenant as the basis for assessing effectiveness in ministry. However, establishing a covenant is not the first step in the implementation of the process. In order for pastor and congregation to make commitments that are appropriate, there must be a basis for determining priorities and goals.

Therefore, the first step in the ministry assessment and evaluation process is for the covenant partners to assess their unique gifts, to know their neighbors, and to discern how they are being called to participate in God's transforming work in that place. *The Book of Discipline* spells out the expectations for the staff-parish relations committee in this regard: "In conducting its work, the committee shall identify and clarify its values for ministry. It shall engage in biblical and theological reflections on the mission of the church, the primary task, and ministries of the local church."[2]

The importance of knowing the context for ministry cannot be overstated. Without it, there is a high risk of setting goals that are irrelevant. There is a danger of establishing a covenant that is not based on a shared vision and that undermines mutual ministry between pastor and laity. It becomes quite likely that goals will be set that are parochial and shortsighted. Churches that establish goals without regard for the needs and assets of the community in which they are located set themselves up for programs of maintenance and survival, which ultimately lead to decay and decline.

Unfortunately, it is not uncommon for local churches to disregard their unique settings and to attempt to carry out ministry as if their surroundings did not matter. Nor is it unusual for pastors to try to replicate what was successful in one congregation as they move from one church to another, not realizing that what was meaningful in one context may not be what is needed in another. One ministry is not necessarily appropriate for all contexts.

Thus, the essential first step in the ministry assessment process must be to know the context in which goals are to be set.

In situations where this work has not been done, the pastor and the staff-parish relations committee will need to take the initiative by requesting that the congregation engage with the pastor in this process of learning about the unique gifts and needs within the church and the community, in considering the wider mission of The United Methodist Church and the annual conference, and in discerning how God is calling them to be in ministry in their unique setting.

This process should include but not be limited to Bible study, gifts assessment, demographic study of the community, walks through the church neighborhood, interviews with church and community leaders, congregational listening sessions, review of the annual conference vision and mission, and input from the district superintendent regarding the cabinet's vision for this local church. The work of John Vincent in situational analysis provides an excellent guide for accomplishing this step in the process (see Appendix A, pp. 59–66).

Knowing the context for ministry is the foundation upon which the church and the pastor can create a covenant and set ministry goals together. With this understanding, the covenant partners are ready to move to the next step in the process.

STEP 2: ESTABLISH A MINISTRY COVENANT.

The pastor and staff-parish relations committee will establish a ministry covenant. A covenant implies *partnership*. The process outlined here, involving the district superintendent, the staff-parish relations committee, and the pastor, assumes the unity of our ministry in Christ, spelled out in *The Book of Discipline*: "The ministry of all Christians is complementary. No ministry is subservient to another. All United Methodists are summoned and sent by Christ to live and work together in mutual interdependence. . . ."[3]

Each of the covenant partners has an important role to play in the process. The covenant requires all partners to take responsibility for creating and fulfilling the covenant. Although the *district superintendent* is not on site in the day-to-day events and the encounters of the congregation, he or she plays a key role in the formation and fulfillment of the covenant. The superintendent provides clear input regarding any cabinet expectations for ministry in light of the mission of the annual conference. It is the superintendent's responsibility to communicate standards and expectations regarding the process, timelines, and reports for ministry assessment and evaluation, and to state how evaluation reports will be used. The district superintendent, with the board of ordained ministry, must also make provision for the training of the staff-parish relations committee, which would include a review of the process for ministry assessment and evaluation. The relationship and communication between the staff-parish relations committee and the district superintendent, as well as with the pastor, are crucial in supporting a fruitful ministry.

The *pastor* and the *staff-parish relations committee* are the covenant partners who will have regular contact as the covenant commitments are carried out in the ongoing ministries of the church. The pastor and committee members should take time to talk about how they understand the relationship that a covenant creates and what mutual ministry means. Reading and reflecting on 1 Corinthians 12 and/or Ephesians 4 is one way to help focus this conversation. A review and discussion of Wesley's theology and the importance of covenant partners in Chapter 1 and Chapter 2 will lay the groundwork for the establishment of the ministry covenant.

The covenant should also include but not be limited to the following:

- Pastor's goals, based upon the vision and mission of the

annual conference, the local church's vision and mission for reaching out to the community and the world, and the pastor's unique gifts. These goals should be written and mutually agreed on by the pastor, the committee, and the district superintendent. The goals will provide the basis for the annual evaluation or "formalization of feedback."

- Provisions for periodic feedback (*How often will the staff-parish relations committee and the pastor meet? Who will have responsibility for convening the meetings?*)
- An agreement about confidentiality
- A process for the annual evaluation or formalization of feedback
- An identification of persons who will receive copies of reports
- A statement of the ways the staff-parish relations committee will support the pastor in accomplishing goals
- A list of other expectations and agreements regarding ministry performance
- In cross-racial or cross-cultural appointments, steps that will be taken to foster understanding and appreciation of cultural and racial differences, especially as they pertain to feedback and evaluation
- A process for handling concerns or conflicts ("The Rule of Christ for the Church," by Terry Gladstone and "Engage Conflict Well" [JustPeace] are excellent guides for staff-parish relations committees in handling grievances and conflicts. See "Suggested Resources" [pp. 53-55]).

The covenant should be dated and signed by the chairperson of the staff-parish relations committee and the pastor and a copy given to the district superintendent. See "Sample Covenant Components" (Appendix C, pp. 69–70).

STEP 3: GIVE AND RECEIVE REGULAR FEEDBACK.

Regular feedback provides a way to affirm and celebrate what is going well, offer or request help as needed, surface and address areas of concern, and make adjustments to the covenant as new circumstances necessitate. It is the means by which the covenant partners can support and hold one another accountable for the fulfillment of the ministries to which they have committed themselves.

The Book of Discipline states: "The [staff-parish relations] committee shall meet at least quarterly. It shall meet additionally at the request of the bishop, the district superintendent, the pastor, any other person accountable to the committee, or the chairperson of the committee."[4] More frequent meetings would be beneficial, especially in the first year of a new appointment.

Pastor and committee members should remember that the purpose of sharing feedback is to assist one another in learning. Conversations in which feedback is shared are times of holy conferencing. They require preparation, adequate uninterrupted time, and a setting that is conducive to thoughtful and unhurried reflection.

The manner in which feedback is given will affect how it is received. Refer to the "Rules for Feedback" (Appendix D, pp. 71–73). Discuss these rules with the pastor and members of the staff-parish relations committee, and consider adopting these as guidelines for giving feedback. Review these rules from time to time, especially before feedback sessions. Monitor performance in adhering to them by checking with one another about how feedback was experienced.

It is not only essential that feedback be given in a way that it can be received but also that it be listened to in way that it can be heard and processed by the one to whom it is given. The questions in "Receiving Feedback: Sample Questions to Assist in Hearing and Processing Feedback" (Appendix E, pp. 74–75) are meant to assist in this process.

STEP 4: FORMALIZE FEEDBACK THROUGH EVALUATION.

Included among the duties of the staff-parish relations committee is the responsibility to "provide evaluation at least annually for the use of the pastor(s) and staff in an ongoing effective ministry and for identifying continuing education needs and plans."[5]

Although the evaluation or "formalization of feedback" is done annually, it is part of the larger ministry assessment process. Understanding that evaluation is just one step in an ongoing process is critical to the integrity of the process and to the usefulness of the feedback. Evaluation involves seven aspects carried out in sequence.

1. Review the Covenant.

The process of evaluation should begin by reviewing the covenant within a previously agreed-upon time frame. The pastor and the members of the staff-parish relations committee should be familiar with the covenant, since they mutually created the covenant and the covenant forms the basis for the ongoing ministry of support and accountability. However, it is wise to review it again before beginning the formal evaluation to ensure that all of the partners in the covenant are reminded of the goals and commitments that were made by the pastor and the committee. These written commitments form the basis for determining what will be evaluated.

2. The Pastor Conducts a Self-Assessment.

Assessment is most useful when it is a self-initiated process of reflecting and listening. It is an opportunity for the pastor to reflect on his or her practice of ministry in relation to the commitments and goals that were jointly agreed upon with the staff-parish relations committee and to consider what is most essential for his or her future ministry. See "Sample Questions for Use in Pastor's Self-Assessment" (Appendix F, pp. 76–77).

Upon completion of the self-assessment, the pastor discusses his or her written reflections with the staff-parish relations committee. This document provides the starting point for the evaluation. (Remember: These conversations are confidential and should not be discussed with anyone outside the committee. Copies of the pastor's self-assessment should be distributed at the beginning of the meeting and collected by the chairperson before adjournment.) If the committee and the pastor agree that it would be helpful, the members of the committee could meet without the pastor to review the pastor's self-assessment in order to prepare to share their feedback. Otherwise, the committee will need to do this with the pastor or the district superintendent present. *The Book of Discipline* is clear:

> The committee shall meet only with the knowledge of the pastor and/or the district superintendent. The pastor shall be present at each meeting of the committee on pastor-parish relations or staff-parish relations except where he or she voluntarily excuses himself or herself. The committee may meet with the district superintendent without the pastor or appointed staff under consideration being present. However, the pastor or appointed staff under consideration shall be notified prior to such meeting with the district superintendent and be brought into consultation immediately thereafter. The committee shall meet in closed session, and information shared in the committee shall be confidential.[6]

3. The Pastor and Staff-Parish Relations Committee
   Share Feedback.

The staff-parish relations committee will meet with the pastor to share feedback regarding the goals outlined in the ministry covenant. A helpful way to begin the conversation with the pastor is for members of the committee to share their points of agreement with the pastor's self-assessment. The committee might then discuss points of disagreement or raise relevant points that are not included in the pastor's self-reflection.

It is useful during the conversation to have a group recorder, who can read back to the group the key points that have been raised during the session. This is a good way of checking whether everyone has heard the same thing or anything has been left out. These notes should be reviewed at the end of the meeting to determine whether all persons are in agreement or any critical points of disagreement should be noted. The recorder's notes will assist the chairperson in writing a summary of the feedback.

4. The Staff-Parish Relations Committee Conducts
   a Self-Assessment.

Feedback and learning is not a one-way proposition. The staff-parish relations committee needs to assess its performance in relation to the covenant commitments made with the pastor and to reflect on how the covenant was maintained in the evaluation process. Questions for the committee to consider include the following:

- What would we change about our covenant?
- What would we change about our process?

The pastor should also be invited to give feedback to the committee regarding his or her experience of the committee's performance in keeping the mutually agreed-upon covenant. One member of the committee may serve as recorder for this portion of the evaluation and summarize reflections, as discussed above. Refer to "Sample Questions for Staff-Parish Relations Committee's Self-Assessment" (Appendix G, p. 78).

5. The Staff-Parish Relations Committee Prepares a Summary.

A summary of the evaluation is to be written by the chairperson of the staff-parish relations committee. This summary should be reviewed with the pastor at a scheduled meeting of the committee, affirmed or amended, and signed by the chairperson of the staff-parish relations committee and the pastor. A copy of the summary should be given to the district superintendent. See "Sample Staff-Parish Relations Committee Summary" (Appendix H, p. 79).

In situations in which the pastor and the staff-parish relations committee have strongly divergent views regarding the fulfillment of the ministry covenant, the committee and the pastor may need to explore options for working through the areas of concern. In some situations, a meeting with the district superintendent may be advisable; but most committees and pastors are capable of working through even very difficult issues when all of the partners are working together. In fact, working through trouble spots can serve to strengthen the team and the ministry. The pastor, the chairperson of the staff-parish relations committee, or the district superintendent may initiate a meeting with the superintendent if such action is determined to be best for the pastor or the church.

6. Use Feedback for Planning Continuing Education.

The *Book of Discipline* makes provision for continuing education and formation for full members and pastors. Note that all of the covenant partners share in the responsibility for supporting this continuous process.

> The pastors in local churches shall participate annually in an evaluation with the committee on pastor-parish relations for use in an ongoing effective ministry and for identifying continuing education needs and plans (¶ 258.2g[5]), using criteria, processes, and training developed by the Board of Ordained Ministry and the cabinet.[7]
>
> Clergy shall be asked by the district superintendent in the charge conference to report on their programs of continuing education, formation, and spiritual growth for the past year and plans for the year to come. The district superintendent shall also ask the local church to describe its provision for time and financial support of continuing education for ministry, professional development, formation and spiritual growth for the pastors, diaconal ministers and deacons serving their primary appointment in that local church.[8]

The duties of the staff-parish relations committee include the following:

> To consult with the pastor and staff concerning continuing education and spiritual renewal, to arrange with the church council for the necessary time and financial assistance for the attendance of the pastor and/or staff at such continuing education and spiritual renewal events as may serve their professional and spiritual growth, and to encourage staff members to seek professional certification in their fields of specialization.[9]

By using feedback from sessions with the staff-parish relations committee and the district superintendent, as well as the self-assessment and input from other sources, areas for continuing education can be identified and goals for continuing education set. A learning objective should answer what the pastor wants to learn and for what purpose. Stating the objective in specific terms makes it easier to select appropriate methods and resources and to determine when learning goals have been achieved and how new learning has been applied. A program for continuing education should include a plan for sharing what has been learned with the staff-parish relations committee, the district superintendent, and the charge conference.

7. Renew the Covenant.

The annual formalization of feedback in the ministry assessment process is a source of valuable learning for the pastor, the staff-parish relations committee, and the district superintendent. It is extremely important at this stage to take time to identify and to talk about what the covenant partners have learned about themselves, about the ministries they have shared, and about their processes of support and accountability. Thoughtful reflection and articulation of new learning will help shape the covenant for the year ahead.

Remember that the covenant must be reviewed and renewed annually. In a year's time, the local church, the surrounding community, the annual conference, the composition of the committee, and the pastor will have changed (even if a new pastor is not appointed). The covenant is a living document; it too must change as relationships and needs for ministry change. Only in this way can it provide mutual support and accountability for persons and the ministries they are called to perform.

EVALUATION OF THE CONGREGATION

After reading the four assessment steps above, one may wonder, "What about the performance of the congregation in fulfilling its commitments?" Is the congregation held accountable in this process? How does this happen? What relevance does the congregation's practice of ministry have for the pastor's performance? These are important questions.

The statement of purpose for the church council in *The Book of Discipline* includes provision for annual evaluation of the mission and ministry of the congregation:

> The **church council** shall provide for planning and implementing a program of nurture, outreach, witness, and resources in the local church. It shall also provide for the administration of its organization and temporal life. It shall envision, plan, implement, and annually evaluate the mission and ministry of the church. The church council shall be amenable to and function as the administrative agency of the charge conference (¶244).[10]

Although not carried out in conjunction with the evaluation of the pastor, this annual assessment by the congregation is essential to a comprehensive ministry assessment. In a covenant-based process of ministry assessment, the evaluation of the pastor is incomplete until the church council has thoughtfully reflected upon its practice of ministry in relation to the church's vision, mission, and goals and has celebrated accomplishments and identified areas of growth. Without the council's evaluation, mutual ministry between laity and clergy is compromised. The evaluation of the congregation would include input from the pastor, church members, and the district superintendent. The charge conference should provide a time for a local church to review its accomplishments and to discuss goals for the coming year.

ASSESSMENT OF THE DISTRICT SUPERINTENDENT'S ROLE

The district superintendent is a partner in the ministry

covenants of all the local churches under his or her charge. Charge conferences, meetings with staff-parish relations committees, one-to-one conferences, and meetings with the district committee on superintendency provide opportunities for the district superintendent to reflect on his or her practice of ministry in relation to the covenant commitments and to invite feedback from pastors and local churches. While specific practices may vary from one annual conference or district to another, district superintendents should be intentional in creating opportunities for reflecting upon their ministry and for receiving meaningful feedback.

TRAINING FOR STAFF-PARISH RELATIONS COMMITTEES AND PASTORS

The cabinet and the board of ordained ministry share the responsibility of equipping staff-parish relations committees for their ministry of evaluation. Changes in the composition of the committee and in pastoral leadership require that such training be offered at regular intervals. Training for staff-parish relations committees and pastors in this ministry assessment model is not difficult and will go a long way in equipping leaders for this crucial ministry. See "Outline for Training Staff-Parish Relations Committees and Pastors" (Appendix I, pp. 80–81).

APPLICATION TO OTHER SETTINGS

As was stated earlier in the book, the process for ministry assessment and evaluation offered here can be most clearly described in relation to a particular minister (or entity) and within a specific ministry setting. The ministry setting depicted here is the local church, and the pastor's ministry performance is the focus of the assessment and evaluation. The covenant partners are the staff-parish relations committee, the pastor, and the district superintendent. While this book describes the process and the covenant partners for a local church setting, the principles and steps outlined are applicable and adaptable to a variety of settings and can be used with a wide range of covenant partners.

Ministry setting, covenant partners, and specific goals and covenantal agreements may vary. Yet the essential components and steps in the process remain the same. No matter where persons serve, what credentials they have, what authority they have been given, or what position they hold—all need to be supported and held accountable for growth in ministry competence.

Consider the following practices. What would happen if they were more the rule than the exception?

- Bishops are required to establish written covenants with the committee on the episcopacy as well as with a group of peers for the purpose of accountability and support in their ministries. What if bishops met with these groups to engage in conversation about their practice of ministry, to reflect on the mission of the annual conference, to share a self-assessment of their effectiveness, and to reflect with the committee on its faithfulness in its ministry of support and accountability?

- District superintendents are required to establish written covenants with the committee on the district superintendency. This would include goals for the superintendent and the committee and would form the basis for an annual review to be shared with the bishop. The committee would meet four times a year to reflect with the superintendent on his or her ministry, to give and receive feedback, and to listen to the superintendent's observations, joys, and struggles in ministry. Written ministry reflection papers from the superintendent's experience (excluding matters that are confidential) could be shared with the committee, with an invitation for the committee members' feedback. Feedback would be formalized in an annual evaluation of the superintendent's and the committee's faithfulness to the covenant; and together they would renew the covenant for the coming year.

- Committees within local churches establish covenants with one another in which they explicitly state their purpose, the assumptions and beliefs about their ministry, and their goals for the year, as well as establish ground rules for their work together. What if committees checked in with one another at the end of each meeting to assess what went well and what needs improvement? What if once a year all committees in the church assessed their effectiveness in upholding the covenant?

- Cabinets establish covenants with mutual understandings about the appointment process and share the document with clergy and staff-parish relations committees, with an invitation for them to respond. This could include a number of shared expectations regarding appointment updates for clergy, consultation with staff-parish relations committees, the process for announcing pastoral appointment changes, procedures that will be followed if a pastor or local church says no to an appointment, etc.

- The examination process for ministry candidates begins with the candidate's self-assessment based upon shared expectations and the accomplishment of agreed-upon areas of growth. The development of relationships, disciplines, and structures of support and accountability for ongoing theological reflection and learning are required for all ministry candidates and expected after ordination or licensing.

Evaluation of the Ministry Assessment Process

If it is to be true to the principles upon which it is based, this process of ministry assessment, like any other practice, must itself be subjected to evaluation. So, regularly evaluate the process and the way it is implemented in order to make improvements. Through ongoing and systematic reflection upon this practice, the church will continue to learn and to grow in its ability to carry out the ministry of ministry assessment.

Notes

1. *The Book of Discipline of The United Methodist Church—2008* (Nashville: The United Methodist Publishing House, 2008), ¶104, p. 76.
2. Ibid., ¶258.2, p. 180.
3. Ibid., ¶130, p. 90.
4. Ibid., ¶258.2e, p. 181.
5. Ibid., ¶258.2g (5), p. 182.
6. Ibid., ¶ 258.2e, p. 181.
7. Ibid., ¶ 350.1, p. 267.
8. Ibid., ¶ 351.5, p. 268.
9. Ibid., ¶258.2g (8), p. 182.
10. Ibid., ¶252.1, p. 167.

Conclusion

"No motif in the Wesleyan tradition has been more constant than the link between Christian doctrine and Christian living. Methodists have always been strictly enjoined to maintain the unity of faith and good works through the means of grace, as seen in John Wesley's *Nature, Design, and General Rules of the United Societies* (1743). The coherence of faith with ministries of love forms the discipline of Wesleyan spirituality and Christian discipleship."[1]

This book is offered in response to an expressed need for a way to hold together support and accountability in the practice of ministry so that we might be continually transformed by the grace of God and become more completely the body of Christ. It is born of the conviction that support and accountability belong together—one cannot exist without the other. And both are essential for the faithful living out of the gospel. This process is an attempt to provide a method for rooting the ministry of ministry assessment and evaluation in a Wesleyan theological framework.

"The coherence of faith with ministries of love" comes through a process of growing and learning and ongoing transformation. Covenant-making and covenant-keeping support this growth by providing a way for Christian disciples to "watch over one another in love." It offers a method for supporting and holding one another accountable as each one seeks to be faithful to the specific commitments that he or she has made for fruitfulness in ministry in response to God's grace.

As mentioned in the previous chapter, the reader is encouraged to consider how this process can be adapted for use in a variety of ministry settings. For example, how might this covenantal process be used by boards of ordained ministry in the preparation and examination of candidates seeking to be ordained? Might the use of a covenant that encompasses the Disciplinary requirements and is reviewed with the covenant partners create a sense of joint ownership and responsibility for both the process and the decisions, without compromising a board's responsibility for recommending candidates for ministry?

How might this process be adapted for committees on the episcopacy and their bishops, district committees on superintendency and their district superintendents, and general agencies and their staff? What would it mean for the church if written covenants and holy conferencing regarding the fulfillment of covenantal commitments formed the basis for interagency relationships?

Covenant-making and covenant-keeping need not be limited to use with clergy and staff. Whether laypersons or pastors, paid or volunteer staff—all need to be supported and held accountable for Christian discipleship. By incorporating the practice of covenant-making into all aspects of church life and ministry, including church committees, task forces, ministry teams, and classes, we will become more like the community Paul describes in his letter to the Ephesians (4:15-16):

> Speaking the truth in love, we must grow up in every way into him who is the head, into Christ, from whom the whole body, joined and knit together by every ligament with which it is equipped, as each part is working properly, promotes the body's growth in building itself up in love.

Notes

1. *The Book of Discipline of The United Methodist Church—2008* (Nashville: The United Methodist Publishing House, 2008), ¶101, p. 48.

Suggested Resources

LEADERSHIP, SUPERVISION, EVALUATION

The Alban Institute, 2121 Cooperative Way, Suite 100, Herndon, VA 20171; Web site: *www.alban.org*

The Lewis Center for Church Leadership, Wesley Theological Seminary, 4500 Massachussetts Ave., NW, Washington, DC 20016; Web site: *www.churchleadership.com*

The Pohly Center for Supervision and Leadership Formation, United Theological Seminary, 4501 Denlinger Road, Dayton, OH 45426; Web site: *www.united.edu* (Click on "Lifelong Learning" and then on "Pohly Center for Supervision and Leadership Formation.")

CONFLICT

Gladstone, Terry N. "The Rule of Christ for the Church: A Manual for the Pastor Parish Relations Committee." E-mail:

DeaconTery@aol.com; telephone: 800-344-0544

JustPeace: Center for Mediation and Conflict Transformation; Web site: *www.justpeaceumc.org*

CROSS-CULTURAL–CROSS-RACIAL CLERGY APPOINTMENTS

Lyght, Ernest S., Glory E. Dharmaraj, and Jacob S. Dharmaraj. *Many Faces, One Church: A Manual for Cross-Racial and Cross-Cultural Ministry*. Nashville: Abingdon Press, 2006.

McSpadden, Lucia Ann. *Meeting God at the Boundaries: Cross-Cultural–Cross-Racial Clergy Appointments*. Nashville: General Board of Higher Education and Ministry, The United Methodist Church, 2003.

_____ *Meeting God at the Boundaries: A Manual for Church Leaders*. Nashville: General Board of Higher Education and Ministry, The United Methodist Church, 2006.

WESLEYAN THEOLOGY

Carder, Kenneth L. *Living Our Beliefs*. Nashville: Discipleship Resources, 1998.

Maddox, Randy L. *Responsible Grace: John Wesley's Practical Theology*. Nashville: Kingswood Books, 1994.

Knight, Henry H. *The Presence of God in the Christian Life: John Wesley and the Means of Grace*. Metuchen, NJ: Scarecrow Press, 1992.

Runyon, Theodore. *The New Creation: John Wesley's Theology Today*. Nashville: Abingdon Press, 1998.

CONTEXT FOR MINISTRY

General Board of Higher Education and Ministry, 1001 Nineteenth Avenue, South, Nashville, TN 37203; Web site: *www.gbhem.org*

General Board of Global Ministries, 475 Riverside Drive, New York, NY 10115; Web site: *gbgm-umc.org/global*

General Board of Discipleship, 1908 Grand Avenue, Nashville, TN 37203; (877) 899-2780; Web site: *www.gbod.org*

Appendices

Situation Analysis*

Assign a group (no more than 12 persons) in the congregation to do a situation analysis using informal and formal methods of analysis and following the steps outlined below:

METHODS

Informal Methods—Listen and Loiter

Hanging around favorite spots; talking outside schools, in shops, in laundromats, at welfare offices, at clinics, etc.; observing and listening in places where people gather and converse; finding those to whom people turn for help; getting into the culture of the community.

Formal Methods—Data and Research

Surveys, questionnaires, census data, household surveys, interviews, conversations, group work, photographs, films, audiovisual recordings, histories, newspapers, demographic studies.

STEPS

Step 1: Start.

Create two "Top Ten" lists, one of "things for joy" and another of "things for sorrow." What in your community and church gives you joy, and what gives you sorrow? After each list has been compiled, discuss and sort to establish priorities.

Step 2: Mark Your Place.

On a map of your area, and using a consistent color system, mark key features such as the following:

Roads and Transportation

The road network can be shown at three levels: (a) major roads, such as commuter and transportation routes; important town or neighborhood roads; (b) other streets, mainly residential access roads; (c) bus stops, subways, etc.

Buildings and Facilities

Mark churches, parks, public buildings, shops, schools, etc. Where are the focal points?

Housing

Mark housing by color to distinguish between privately owned houses, rental property, single-family houses, multifamily houses, high-rise accommodations, etc.

Residents

Locate predominant residential groupings and mark the areas where they live. For example: Elderly Residents (ER); Young Families (YF); Middle Aged (MA); Single (S)

Ethnic Groups

Indicate where there is a clear predominance of particular ethnic/racial groups. What languages are spoken?

Demolition Areas

Identify waste sites and demolished or condemned buildings.

Assets

What assets exist in your community? Examples may include economic, spiritual, and educational leadership, cultural and racial diversity, land, recreational facilities, healthcare institutions.

Other Features

Indicate and label other significant features of the neighborhood on the map. Use your imagination about what to include.

Step 3: Write About Your Community.

Supplement the map with brief, written details on the following, comparing your areas with the national/state/county averages:

People

- Who are they? Are they elderly, middle aged, young families, children, single?
- What sort of jobs do they have? Where do they work?
- Why are they there? (choice? coercion?)
- How long have they been there? (stability/mobility)
- What do they look for outside the area?
- Where do they come from? (places of birth and upbringing)
- How ethnically diverse are they?
- Do most people own a car?
- What is the unemployment level?

- How big is the total population?
- Who is not represented in the community?

Relationships

- What do people do together? (for example, institutions, clubs, associations, local politics, informal groups)
- Who is respected, feared, considered significant? Why?
- How do people get along with one another, within groups, and between groups?

Perceptions

- How is the place seen by the residents?
- How is the place seen by people from outside the area? by the professionals (planners, estate agents, social workers, police, teachers, clergy)? by you?
- How do the residents see other places and outsiders?
- What myths exist about the area?
- What do people complain about?
- What are people proud of or pleased about?

Recent Experiences

- When have the people acted together to achieve something?
- Which people have acted? Did they act to change or to preserve the status quo?
- Is anyone trying to identify the needs and potential of the community?
- Who is determining the shape of your community? Who are the people making the decisions?
- What groups or people, parties, or departments impose their will on the community?

- What changes have you seen in your area? Who made them? Who opposed them?
- What attitudes did or does your church have toward these movements or developments?

Lifestyle

- What conflicts of lifestyle are there in the community?
- What assumptions and values are indicated by the way groups of people live?
- Are there "top" people and "bottom" people?

Step 4: Describe Your Church.

Provide brief details on the following:

The Situation

- What churches are located in your area?
- What are your church's ecclesiastical structures and boundaries?
- List the categories of people belonging to your church:
    > Staff, ordained and lay
    > Lay leadership
    > Church attendees by numbers, gender, and age
    > Major residence areas (mark on the map)
    > Fringe members or irregular attendees

The Activities

Describe your congregation's activities according to the following categories:

- Worship—average worship attendance

- Programs—Sunday school, small groups, outreach groups
- Premises—date of buildings, number of rooms, present condition and use
- Finance—(a) present financial position; (b) next year's budget

Church Members Compared With the Local Community

Compare your congregation's members with the members of the community, using the following indicators:

- Economic status and social position
- Place of origin and mobility
- Cultural interests
- Length of association
- Place of residence
- Age
- Gender
- Race/Ethnicity

Portrait of the Church Community

Construct a profile of your church community, using the criteria below:

- Relationship of the leadership to the congregation
- Number of persons who attend worship services who are also involved in other church activities
- Recent history of the church (buildings, mergers, events, campaigns)
- Decision-making processes (church policies, program, leadership, and budget)
- Involvement of church in wider community

- Involvement of wider community in church events
- Annual conference/district ministries—congregation's involvement in conference, district, and general church mission and ministry; conference, district, and general church resources used by the congregation
- Congregation's involvement in and cooperation with ecumenical efforts
- Relationship of the church with the "stranger"
- Differences and similarities between pastors and congregants about what it means to be the church
- Role of the church school in Christian formation

The Church and the Community

- List other work being done by others within the community (for example, community concern groups, care-of-the-needy groups, advocacy groups) that intersects with the church's mission
- Who holds the power in the community? Are there powerful or powerless people in the community? Both? Who specifically?
- What actions, projects, and institutions in your community is the church supporting?
- What is the church trying to change?
- What actions, groups, and initiatives could the church support? or change?
- What are other churches in your area doing in the community?

Step 5: Move From Analysis to Action.

Review the two Top Ten lists you constructed in Step 1, and consider what your situation analysis may be saying to you and your church about what you could do in your church and your community. How is God calling you and your church to live out the gospel in this context? Share your findings with the church council, the pastor, and the staff-parish relations committee.

*Adapted from "Situation Analysis," in *Diploma in Community Ministry: Tutor's File, Programmes, Presentations and Process*, by John J. Vincent (1973), Urban Theology Unit, 210 Abbeyfield Road, Sheffield S4 7AZ, United Kingdom; revised by Christine Dodd (1991) and Ian K. Diffield (1997). Used by permission.

Appendix B
Steps in Covenant-Making*

(A companion tool to use with Chapter 3)

1. Understand what a covenant is and why covenant-making is relevant to the staff-parish relations committee's work.

2. Consider what a covenant offers a committee.
   • A fresh beginning
   • A theological foundation
   • A structure for growing and improvement
   • A standard for assessment

3. Decide to become a covenantal community/committee.

4. Determine what items to include in the covenant. This will vary from committee to committee. (See "Sample Covenant Components," Appendix C, p. 69–70.)

5. Over a period of one to two months, write a covenant.
   • Work in task groups to gather and bring back information.
   • Work as a whole group to add or revise items for the covenant.
   • Have one person compile the components into a document.
   • Review the document.

6. Formalize the covenant.
   • Ask all the parties to sign the covenant.
   • Celebrate through worship and prayer.
   • Share a copy with the district superintendent.

7. Work on covenant-keeping.
   - Read the covenant at the beginning or end of each meeting.
   - Review the covenant periodically at meetings.
   - Keep a copy of the covenant on display.
   - Be sure that new members of the committee understand and accept the covenant. (A good time to review the covenant and to consider what changes, if any, need to be made to the covenant is when a new member joins the group.)

8. Conduct an annual self-assessment of the committee's work in light of the covenant.

9. Revise the covenant as necessary; but do so at least annually, and more often, if necessary.

* Pohly Center for Supervision and Leadership Formation, United Theological Seminary, Dayton, Ohio. Used by permission.

Sample Covenant Components
(See Chapter 3, pp. 34–36)

We believe: (Include common assumptions and core values.)

Our church's vision/mission statement and goals for the coming year are:

Our annual conference's vision, mission, and critical issues are:

Our pastor's goals, set in consultation with the staff-parish relations committee, are:

The staff-parish relations committee will meet with the pastor ____ times per year to provide feedback regarding his or her practice.

We will engage in evaluation with the pastor annually, using the following process:

We will assess our process and performance in the fulfillment of our covenant by:

We will use the following agreed-upon guidelines for handling grievances, concerns, or conflicts:

We will observe the following guidelines for our meetings:

We will intentionally reflect on how God is present through our work.

Other commitments include:

Signed _____ Date _____
_____ *Pastor* _____

Signed _____ Date _____
_____ *Chairperson, Staff-Parish* _____
_____ *Relations Committee* _____

Signed _____ Date _____
_____ *District Superintendent* _____

Rules for Feedback*

Focus on behaviors (what the person did) or outcomes (what resulted). Do not focus on traits (for example, "helpful," "cooperative"). For example, don't say, "You are an inspirational pastor." While such global comments may sound nice, they don't provide the pastor with specific, helpful feedback. Rather, you might say, "The staff-parish relations committee particularly appreciates the way you relate Scripture lessons to contemporary issues. For example, your sermon on the forgiveness of Jesus and its application to dealing with unfairness in our daily lives was particularly inspirational."

Give "I" or "We" messages and avoid characterizations. For example, rather than saying, "You are too indifferent in dealing with parishioners' personal problems," you could say, "When you tell parishioners that you are too busy to meet with them, we (they) feel that you don't care." The first statement is a generalization and tends to evoke a defensive reaction. The second approach speaks about a specific action and does not characterize the person as being indifferent. It expresses your feelings, and it invites the person to respond rather than to argue.

Be specific in providing feedback. Most people require specific examples in order to correct or reinforce their behaviors.

Be honest in providing feedback. Feedback should not be used to manipulate or to pacify.

Confine feedback narrowly to the behaviors that affect you as the parish or that are appropriately within your role as a parishioner. For example, don't comment on the way the pastor fulfills his or her role as a parent. This is not the business of the staff-parish relations committee, unless it has immediate and direct implications for the church.

Describe behaviors or outcomes and your reaction to them. Effective feedback is descriptive; it does not label behavior as good or bad.

Time feedback well so as to be constructive and informative, rather than destructive or embarrassing.

Direct feedback toward behaviors that the receiver can reinforce or change.

Deliver feedback in an appropriate balance of positive and negative.

Provide feedback on a frequent basis. It should be an ongoing activity, not a once-a-year event.

Be sure that feedback is a two-way process.

Remember the following when you hear a grievance about the pastor:

- Do not rely on hearsay (if possible), and never simply relay anonymous information.
- Realize that what makes one person unhappy may be precisely what another person likes about the pastor.
- Don't assume that if a need is not being met, it is the pastor's fault. Engage the pastor in dialogue as part of

the regular communication process. If need be, the concern should be raised again in the annual formalization of feedback process.

References

Lathan, G.P. and Wexley, K.N. *Increasing Productivity Through Performance Appraisal.* Reading, MA: Addison and Wesley Publishing Co., 1982.

Robbins, S.P. *Training in Interpersonal Skills.* Englewood Cliffs, NJ: Prentice Hall, 1989.

Wexley, K.N. and Latham, G.P. *Developing and Training Human Resources in Organizations.* New York: HarperCollins, Inc., 1991.

Whetten, D.A. and Cameron, K.S. *Developing Management Skills.* New York: HarperCollins Publishing Inc., 1993.

*Adapted from workshop materials prepared by Jane Giacobbe-Miller, former chairperson of the staff-parish relations committee, Wesley United Methodist Church, Amherst, Massachusetts, for district training of staff-parish relations committees and pastors in the Central Massachusetts District, New England Conference, The United Methodist Church. Used by permission.

Appendix E

Receiving Feedback:
Sample Questions to Assist in
Hearing and Processing Feedback*

Clarifying Questions

- "Can you give an illustration when you may have observed this happening?"
- "Let me repeat what I think you said to be sure that I am hearing accurately."
- "Am I correct in my understanding that . . . ?"

Decision-Making Questions

- "If we were to change what you have been describing, what would it look like? What would need to be done? Who might do it?"
- "Should I consider dropping this ministry, receive continuing education, or delegate this responsibility to someone else?"
- "Are my feelings/perceptions/observations on target? Are they an appropriate guide for future decisions?"

Consensus-Testing Questions

In instances where only one person has contributed an idea:

I respect Mary's opinion about this, and I would like to go with her insight. But before I do, I need to hear what others of you think about this. To what extent does her opinion represent yours ideas?

In instances where other members of the congregation have been quoted:

> I would be interested to know whether others on the committee have also heard this report and from how many persons. Do the persons you have heard from represent a particular group within the church; for example, young adults, the choir, the trustees, etc.?

*These questions are from Richard Yeager, ed., *Developing and Evaluating an Effective Ministry: A Manual for Pastors and Diaconal Ministers* (Nashville: General Board of Higher Education and Ministry, n.d.), 25.

Sample Questions for Use in Pastor's Self-Assessment*

Pastor _____

Position _____

Please complete the following evaluation questions. Use additional pages if needed.

What goals and expected outcomes for your ministry were agreed upon in the covenant between you and the staff-parish relations committee?

What progress have you made toward these goals? (Give specific examples, where possible.)

Are there areas in which you feel that your ministry performance has not met expectations? (Describe.)

What are the possible reasons for not meeting expectations? What steps should be taken to change this?

What have you learned and how have you grown through your experience over the past year?

What specific skills, strengths, and interests do you feel you have demonstrated that should be more fully utilized in the future?

How can the staff-parish relations committee and/or the district superintendent help you build on these?

What continuing education opportunities do you plan to pursue?

Signed _____ Date _____
                    Pastor

*Adapted from "Employee Evaluation 2002," Belmont United Methodist Church, Nashville, Tennessee. Used by permission.

Sample Questions for Staff-Parish Relations Committee's Self-Assessment

What commitments did the staff-parish relations committee make as part of the covenant with the pastor?

What progress was made toward these goals?

Are there areas where expectations were not met?

What are the possible reasons for not meeting these expectations? What steps should be taken to change this?

What new learning will contribute to your effectiveness as a staff-parish relations committee?

Signed _____ Date _____
Chairperson, Staff-Parish
Relations Committee

Sample Staff-Parish
Relations Committee Summary

Write a brief narrative that includes areas of ministry that were evaluated, the process that was used, and strengths and areas of growth that were identified.

List strengths and areas of growth for the staff-parish relations committee.

List priorities for the pastor's ministry for the coming year (if these have been established).

List recommendations for the coming year (continuing education, additional staff, recruitment of additional lay leadership, training for lay leadership, etc.)

Signed _____ Date _____
Chairperson, Staff-Parish
Relations Committee

Signed _____ Date _____
Pastor

Outline for Training Staff-Parish Relations Committees and Pastors

The outline below is meant to serve as a starting point for designing training for pastors and staff-parish relations committees, using the model for ministry assessment and evaluation presented in this book. The training may be expanded or condensed depending upon the time available and the particular needs of the group. Part II could be offered as a three-hour workshop (including a fifteen-minute break). Parts I, II, and III could be offered as a six- to seven-hour workshop (including a break for lunch and two fifteen-minute breaks). Each participant should have a copy of *Watching Over One Another in Love: A Wesleyan Model for Ministry Assessment* as well as a copy of the paragraphs from the *Book of Discipline* (*BOD*) indicated in the outline. **Note:** Paragraph numbers refer to the 2008 *Book of Discipline*, while page numbers refer to relevant pages in *Watching Over One Another in Love*.

Opening

Welcome
Introductions
What to Expect From This Workshop
Prayer

Part I

Roles and Responsibilities of the Staff-Parish Relations Committee
- Overview (*BOD*, ¶258.2)
- Consultation with the district superintendent in appointment process (*BOD*, ¶¶431-435)

- Consultation with the district superintendent in evaluation (*BOD*, ¶350.1)

Part II
A Wesleyan Model for Ministry Assessment and Evaluation

- Theological Foundations
  - > Salvation by grace is a gradual process (pp. 4-5)
  - > Faith and fruit go together (pp. 6-7)
  - > The means of grace support growth in love (pp. 7-9)
  - > Implications for ministry assessment (pp. 9-12)
- Covenant: A Way of Holding Together Support and Accountability (pp. 15-20)
- The Process
  - > Know the context of ministry (pp. 32-34)
  - > Establish a ministry covenant (pp. 34-36)
  - > Give and receive regular feedback (pp. 37-38)
  - > Formalize feedback through evaluation (pp. 38-43)
  - > Evaluation of the congregation (pp. 43-44)
  - > Evaluation of the ministry assessment process (p. 48)

Part III
A Process for Engaging Conflict

- Using "Engage Conflict Well" and "The Rule of Christ for the Church" as resources, discuss the staff-parish relations committee's role in developing a process for dealing with issues of conflict.

Closing
Questions
Wrap-Up and Evaluation of the Workshop
Sending Forth

CPSIA information can be obtained at www.ICGtesting.com
Printed in the USA
LVOW071258050812

292989LV00002B/5/P